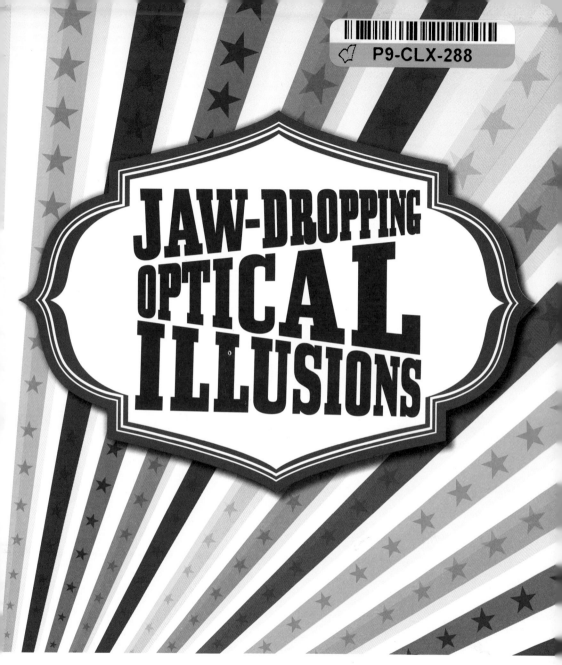

JAW-DROPPING OPTICAL ILLUSIONS

Parragon

Bath · New York · Cologne · Melbourne · Delhi
Hong Kong · Shenzhen · Singapore · Amsterdam

This edition published by Parragon Books Ltd in 2015 and distributed by

Parragon Inc.
440 Park Avenue South, 13th Floor
New York, NY 10016
www.parragon.com

Copyright © Parragon Books Ltd 2015
Written and produced by Any Puzzle Media Ltd

ISBN 978-1-4748-0424-0

Printed in China

Introduction

Prepare to be **amazed** as you begin your journey into the world of optical illusions.

If you think you can tell straight from curved, vertical from angled, or still from moving, you're in for a surprise! Just take a look at the lines below—the red lines seem to bend, but they're really perfectly straight. And this is just the beginning.

At first glance this seems to be a regular nut, but you'd need a very strangely shaped bolt to screw this **_impossible shape_** onto!

Could you make this shape? It might look like a regular triangle, but trace your finger or eye around one of the edges and you'll soon spot **something strange** about it!

JAW-DROPPING OPTICAL ILLUSIONS

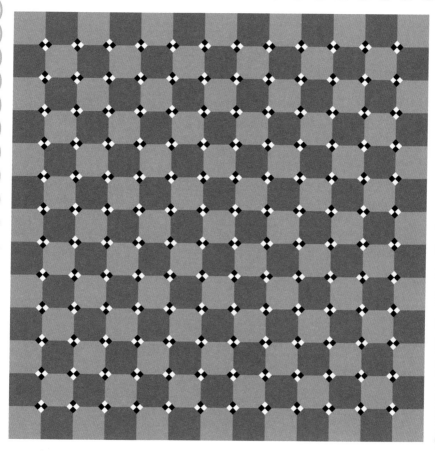

This image appears to bulge, but in fact it consists only of *perfect squares*. The black and white intersecting squares are confusing your brain! Check with a ruler, if you need convincing.

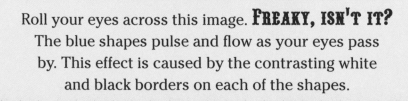

Roll your eyes across this image. **FREAKY, ISN'T IT?**
The blue shapes pulse and flow as your eyes pass
by. This effect is caused by the contrasting white
and black borders on each of the shapes.

Look at the two gray
tiles marked with dots. It's
hard to believe, but *they're both
the **same** shade of gray*!

Don't believe it? Make a small
hole in a piece of paper and
look at the tiles through it.

STARE
into the center
of the book, and
slowly
move it
closer
and
closer
toward you.

The white area
in the center of
the image slowly

larger ... and
larger ... and
larger!

These diagonal lines create a vivid, **flashing** interference pattern. The vertical divisions between each column also appear to bend slightly—although in reality this isn't true.

The central gray strip is **EXACTLY THE SAME COLOR** from top to bottom, yet it appears to change shade. The surrounding grays are influencing your perception.

Stare at the dot in the center of the upper image for 30 seconds, then **rapidly** transfer your focus to the corresponding dot in the lower image. You should briefly see the gray shapes change to a green square and red triangle on top of a yellow background.

On initial inspection this might seem to be an ordinary picture of a vase on a shelf, with a mug hanging below. But take a closer look and you'll see that **all is not as it seems ...**

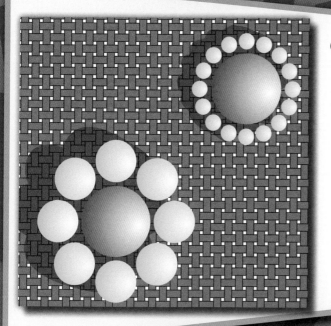

On first inspection these two orange circles appear to be **different sizes**—but they are actually exactly the same! The surrounding circles trick your brain into falsely compensating for "distance."

These two arcs seem to be **different heights**, but they are both the same size!

It might also look like the right-hand curve bends more sharply, but both arcs truly are identical.

As you move your eyes around this strange, red image, it will appear to jump out at you in **SHARP, SUDDEN** forward leaps.

This cat appears to have ***two green eyes***, but it's an optical illusion. If you look closely, the eye on the left is actually completely gray. The surrounding purple hue is responsible for this effect.

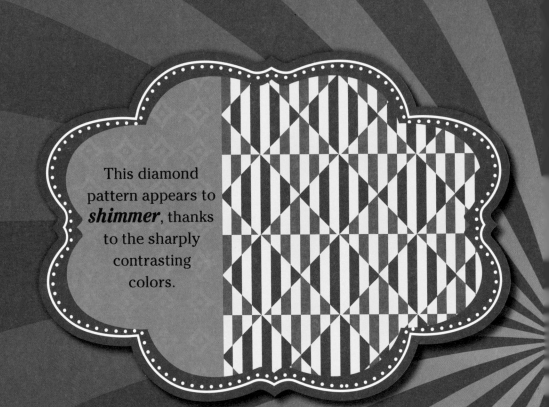

This diamond pattern appears to **_shimmer_**, thanks to the sharply contrasting colors.

The background concentric circles in this image cause the foreground square to appear to bend on each side—when it is in fact a perfect square. This effect was first documented by the psychologist William Orbison in 1939.

The outer triangle in the top image is cut up as shown, and then rearranged as per the bottom picture. When this is done **an extra space appears**, as shown—you can try this with a bit of paper to prove it to yourself!

These rectangles seem to slide around the page, simply *just by looking* at them!

There's **something strange** about this steam engine.
Superficially, this picture looks perfectly plausible,
but if you follow the paths around you'll soon spot
something strange about how they appear to connect …

At first glance this seems to be half a face facing forward. Or is it actually half a face *viewed side-on*?

Is this a silhouette of a man? And if you turn the page **upside down**, what does the white area also look like?

Move your eyes around the image below and you'll see it **sway,** *bulge,* and **move** in all kinds of unexpected ways! Your brain seems to be trying to straighten the curves, and is confused by the strongly contrasting colors.

This central red shape **appears to float** on a higher layer than the black circles surrounding it. This is due to the huge variation in clarity between the two layers.

What would happen if you tried to *turn the upper cog*? Could you actually make this mechanism in reality?

The truth is that you could never build this—the metal frame is impossible, even without considering the cogs.

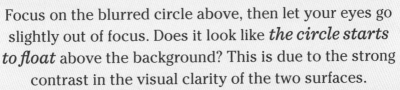

Focus on the blurred circle above, then let your eyes go slightly out of focus. Does it look like *the circle starts to float* above the background? This is due to the strong contrast in the visual clarity of the two surfaces.

This appears to be a drawing of a ***spiral***, winding ever closer to the center of the image. But if you put your finger on the spiral and trace it around the picture, you'll discover that it's actually a series of ***concentric circles***—the spiral is completely illusory!

This juggler has a lot of spheres in the air! Luckily they're only *rotating slowly*, as you can see if you look at them on the page ...

Do you see flickering dots and movement along the **thick** white lines? This is purely a **FIGMENT** of your imagination!

This scintillating grid effect, where dots seem to appear in the grid intersections, is called the *Hermann Grid* after its discovery in the 19th century by German scientist, Ludimar Hermann.

The dice-like pattern below appears to *warp and bend*, but if you use a ruler or other straight edge you'll soon discover that it is in fact all perfectly square!

What is going on in this picture? It looks like a fake perspective image with the man some distance back, but this would require the man's shadow to be behind him, not on the floor near the woman. She must be holding a small doll.

Cover over the parts of this image outside the dashed lines and all four green segments seem to be the same color, but as you can see when you uncover it, they are in fact *different shades*!

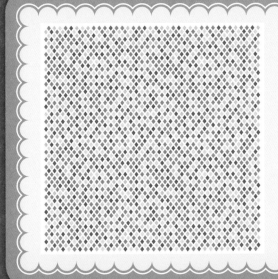

The image on the left consists of randomly colored diamonds, but your brain can't help but **see patterns and even shapes** in it. Your vision system likes to try to make sense of whatever you give it.

Move the book back and forth from left to right and then right to left. Does the circle to the right *appear to float* on top of the background?

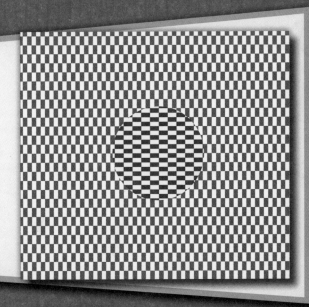

Do these squares appear to be **_rotating_** around the center of the image?

The image to the left is *a perfect rectangle*, believe it or not, and all of the shapes within it are square. It looks like the grid lines are diagonal, but if you use a straight edge you'll see that they're all completely horizontal or vertical.

The height of the lines in the image to the right seem to vary as you travel along the wave, but in fact each of the vertical bars is precisely **the same height**!

This seems to be a modern-looking stair installation, but **there's something wrong** with these green steps. Although they appear to make sense, if you trace around the upper level of the gray blocks you'll see that this arrangement couldn't be built in reality.

The pattern to the right appears to contain **glowing white circles,** but in fact only straight lines are present. Even without the diagonal lines, the effect remains.

This image appears to consist of **a curved mesh**, but once again all of the grid lines run in straight horizontal or vertical lines across the image.

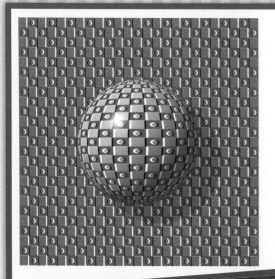

This sphere appears to be *floating in front of the page*, while the background of the picture seems to be slowly floating past.

It might be **hard to believe**, but the shade of blue marked with the arrow at the top is *identical* to the shade of blue marked with the lower arrow!

This fantastic shape looks great on the page, but you would have **trouble building** it in real life! For example, the center cube is beneath the top one, but it's also on the same level if you trace around the blue and green pipes on the top level.

These snakes look like they're **SLITHERING**, thanks to the arrow pattern printed on them!

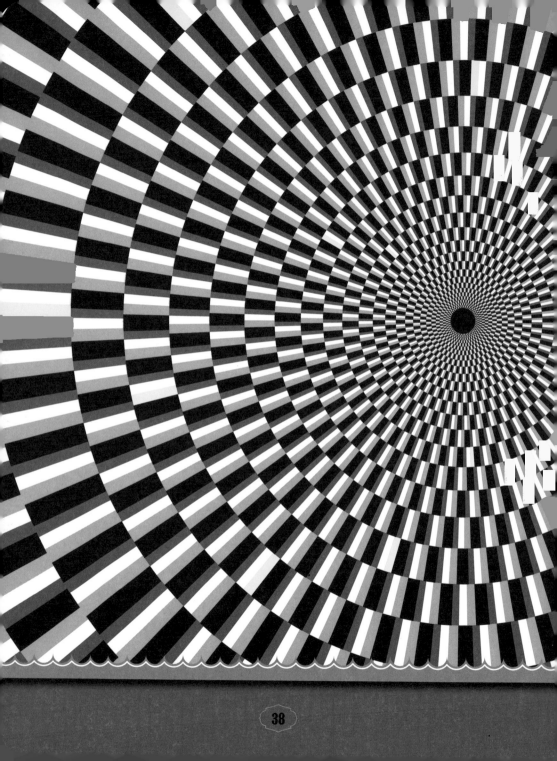

The center of
this image really
does seem to

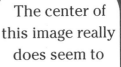

with a nervous
energy—as if
trying to turn,
yet not quite
managing
to move.

This image looks perfectly normal, apart from being upside down. Now try turning the book **upside down** instead. Does it still look normal?

Does the silhouette on the far right of this image *look larger* than the silhouette on the left? It's an optical illusion, caused by the background grid.

This square appears to **warp** in toward the center of the circles, but in reality it is a perfect square with completely straight sides!

These spiky shapes will ***start to swirl*** as you move your eyes diagonally across the page. This effect is caused entirely by the color gradation on each shape.

These two path shapes appear to lean at **very different angles**, but take a closer look and you'll see that in fact they are *identical*! This remarkable illusion works thanks to your brain's autocorrection for the contents of what it assumes must be a real-world view.

If you were to **continue the black line** from the left, which of the colored lines to the right would it end up overlapping? Most people suggest blue or green, but remarkably the answer is in fact the red line.

Are these regular children's wooden blocks, or has something strange happened here? If you look closely, the top of the image bends back in an impossible way!

These black-and-white shapes give the impression of **a tunnel of infinite length**, burrowing down into the page. They also shimmer and distort toward the distant part of the tunnel!

The area inside this shape appears to be *a brighter white* than the white background outside the shape, but in fact this is an illusion—they are both the same color.

The gaps between these posts seem to **get narrower** from left to right, but in fact each gap is exactly the same width!

These rows of shapes appear to be angled, but are in fact completely straight.

Is this a **handprint**—
or is it a silhouette
of two people?

If you look at the top first
you'll see people, but if
you look at the bottom
first you'll see a hand!

The areas around the white lines in this image seem to *glow* brighter than the rest of the page, but it's just an illusion.

Can you spot the **camouflaged** bird in this picture? It's just left of center, with its head raised up to the sky. This bird, a bittern, has subtle brown plumage that blends almost perfectly into its reed-bed habitat. When frightened, it stands perfectly still and points its beak upward to look just like a reed stalk!

WHAT DO YOU SEE when you look at this picture? Is it a yacht on a lake with a fire burning on a hill, or is it a ghostly blue face in the sky looking down on the Earth?

This **watery chasm** has been created on this bridge using just chalk and an understanding of perspective.

If you cut up a square as shown in the top image, then rearrange as per the image below, you end up with *an extra piece* sticking out. That's amazing! It's because the new shape is slightly less tall, so isn't really a square.

Stare at this black-and-white ring arrangement for 20 seconds, then look away at a white surface such as a wall. Do you see an inverted, ***ghostly after-image***?

Do you feel that you are getting

into the very center of the book?

This Escher-esque image would require some **serious climbing skills** if it existed in real life! Escher was a Dutch graphic artist, known for his illustrations that featured impossible architectural constructions.

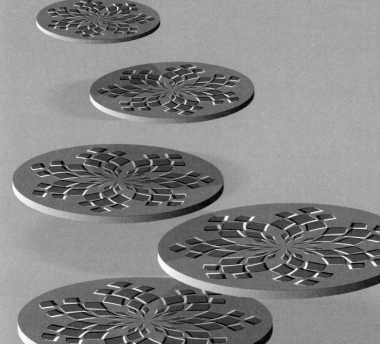

These flying saucers **_appear to spin_** as they travel through the air. This is due to the pattern of white and black markings on the discs.

These tables look **very different**, but the green shapes are actually *identical*—you can measure them with a ruler to prove this!

The thinner-lined junctions in this pattern, which looks like a wall made of cubes, appear to *glow slightly whiter* than the paper color. In fact, all the whites are the same shade.

Stare at the dot in the center of the
upper image for 30 seconds, then rapidly
transfer your gaze to the black dot in
the black-and-white image—which
will now appear in color!

As you look at the center of one of these arrangements of blue shapes, so the three other ones will *seem to rotate*!

This **amazing fractal image** looks so innocent,
but if you look at its center and then slowly
move the page closer and closer to your eyes
you'll discover its more insidious side ...

The image below contains a number of **seemingly plausible**—and yet impossible—connections between surfaces. And that's before you consider the fact that it's magically floating in midair …

The image above has a remarkable **HYPNOTIC** effect. As you move your eyes around the image, look at each of the spiral centers in turn and you'll find that they start to turn—and at different rates, too!

No matter what angle you look at this picture from, the eyes will be looking **_straight back at you_**!

On first inspection this looks like a regular cylinder segment, or a washer—but on closer inspection **the truth is revealed**!

Many creatures have evolved their own **natural optical illusions** to let them blend into their environments. The gray tree frog (*Hyla versicolor*) in this image provides perfect proof of that fact!

It blends in well with the trees, swamps, and ponds which form its natural habitat.

The rings in the shape below appear to be very uneven and far from circular—but each striped ring is in fact *a perfect circle*!

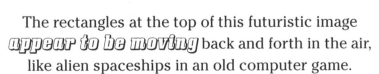

The rectangles at the top of this futuristic image *appear to be moving* back and forth in the air, like alien spaceships in an old computer game.

Look at any dot in the above picture for a second or two, then shift your gaze to another, and so on. You will see ghostly, superbright dots floating in space as you move your eyes around. These are a **persistence of vision** effect.

nassau

The text above, "nassau," is an example of an *ambigram.* In other words, it looks exactly the same when viewed upside down as when viewed right-side-up!

Which of these dots do you think is in the **exact vertical center** of this triangle? Most people choose the middle dot, but amazingly it is in fact the uppermost dot!

These circular patterns seem to **come alive** as you run your eyes over the picture. There is a really strong impression of circular movement.

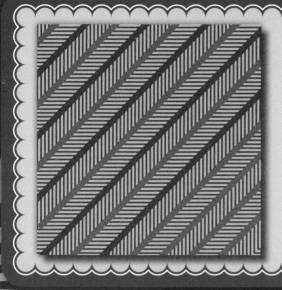

In this pattern the blue and green *lines appear to warp* and bend as they travel across the image. In fact, all of the lines are perfectly straight. The horizontal and vertical lines, despite all being identical, are misleading your brain.

There are only two different designs of row in this tile wall, but even so they seem to *slide around* to try and line themselves up!

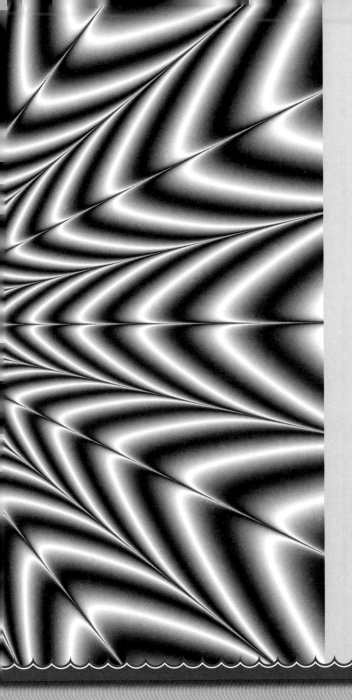

If you're of
a nervous
disposition,
**look
away
now!**

This
shimmering,
vibrating,
energetic,
pulsing,
shining
pattern seems to be
alive on the page.

The alternating colors in this pattern make it very **hard to look at**, encouraging you to look away!

This geometric pattern consists of such strongly contrasting regions that it seems to buzz with **_an invisible energy_**. The effect gets even stronger if you let your eyes go slightly out of focus while looking at it.

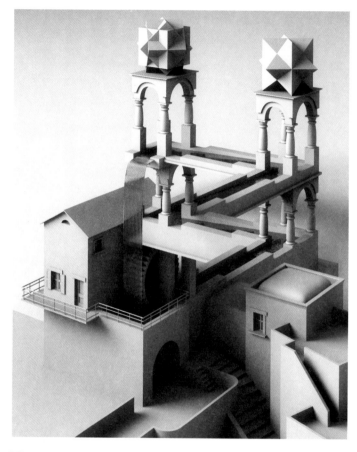

This perpetual-motion waterwheel system would **solve the world's energy needs** if only it could be built in reality! This image is a modern 3-D-model recreation of Escher's classic 1961 *Waterfall* image.

The centers of these shapes create an interesting interference pattern, so they appear to **_flicker very rapidly_** between white and black.

The contrasting shades in this image lead to **phantom colors** appearing. Each semicircle is in fact identical, and the only color used is gray.

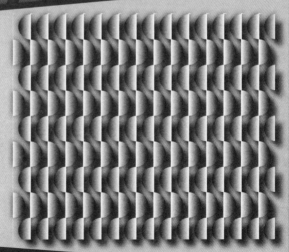

How many **shades of orange** do you see in the image above? In fact, there is only one— the overlapping black-and-white lines contrast so strongly that they affect your perception of the orange.

Which of these two arrows is **_longer_**? Most people would choose the line on the left, but in fact both are exactly the same length! The yellow shape creates a false perspective.

At first glance this seems to be a picture of a woman, but **look a little closer** and you'll see that it is also two crows sitting on a waiter-like mannequin.

This fairground wheel seems to spin all by itself, thanks to the lighting highlights on each of the cars.

This game of *impossible dominoes* would be rather hard to play in reality, but you could certainly have fun trying!

This simple pattern has a most *remarkable effect* on your brain. Without even any shading cues, the columns seem to sway.

If you look at this text and try to see the image to the left out of the edge of your vision, you'll see the shapes start to *slide around* ...

It's hard to tell what lies underneath these circles, but as you try and work it out so the image will ripple and move in a most *disconcerting* way!

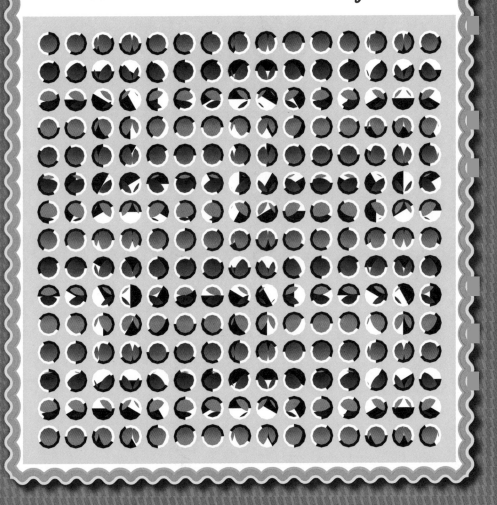

The **yin-yang** symbols appear to orbit the center of the image in a most peaceful way ...

This brass shape *looks rather solid*, but if you tried constructing it you'd find it's anything but! The center shape is somehow both at the back *and* at the front, if you look at its connections.

This arrow points in two directions, that's for sure. Deciding **which two directions** it actually points in, however, is much more difficult to discern!

The **_distance between the points_** of the red and blue arrows seems to be much shorter than the distance between the points of the blue and green arrows— but they are in fact exactly the same length!

This **perspective** drawing, made outside a Dutch office building, appears to show some abstract shapes floating above a garden oasis.

If you fix your eyes on the black dot in the center of this image and then move your head—or the book—slowly closer to the picture, you should see the outer parts of the pattern start to spin.

This effect is called the **Zöllner illusion**, after the German astrophysicist who first discovered that drawing crosshatch marks on parallel lines makes them appear to bend—these lines are in fact all perfectly parallel!

This image appears to contain a yellow star shape, but this is *completely illusory*. It actually consists of many nested yellow squares.

It's said that **"X MARKS THE SPOT"**—but in this case the X itself has more than the average amount of mystery about it! Consider for example the line of the "X" from top-right to bottom-center—it appears aligned, but it's clear from the bottom-right of the shape that this is impossible!

This shape would be as *impossible* to make as the "X" in the image above. If you're not convinced, then just give it a go!

This **classical edifice** could be a remnant of the ancient Greeks ... or at least it could have been, were it not impossible to build! The top of the shape is straight, but the column bases don't match up with this alignment.

These striped lines appear to lean at significant angles, but in fact each runs **perfectly horizontally** across the page.

The paper in the center of these shapes seems to *glow* whiter-than-white, and even slightly brown on the right. Try covering over the surrounding area, however, and this will be revealed as an illusion.

There seem to be **three shades** of each of these vertical strips. In reality, however, each group of three uses only a single color. The effect is caused by the interleaved white and black bars.

What color is the central shape in the image to the right? If you think it's green, then think again! It's actually a perfect gray. The surrounding purple hue misleads the eye.

The fish in this tank seem to **swim back and forth** as you look around the tank. The illusion is created by the striped pattern on each fish.

You wouldn't easily spot this camouflaged butterfly unless you really knew what you were looking for! Only its shadow gives it away.

Is this a zebra with **two bodies**, or just a carefully taken photo?

The circles in the image below seem to be vertically **_misaligned_**, but if you use a ruler you'll discover that they're actually all arranged in a perfectly straight line!

Focus intently on the center of this gray smudge, and you should find that after just a few seconds it starts to fade away. Keep looking at it and it will vanish completely!

This wheel mosaic **doesn't need a motor** to start turning—just looking at it will entirely suffice!

At first sight this looks like a picture of a dove flying through the air. But look a bit closer and you'll see that it's also an angel in flight.

Is this a beautifully sculpted column, **or is it** the silhouette of two people facing one another?

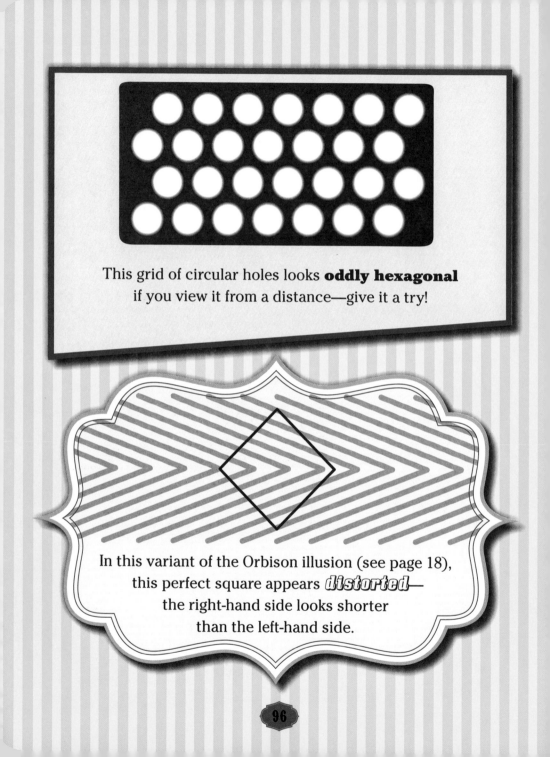

This grid of circular holes looks **oddly hexagonal** if you view it from a distance—give it a try!

In this variant of the Orbison illusion (see page 18), this perfect square appears *distorted*— the right-hand side looks shorter than the left-hand side.

This circle of dots hides **a hidden square**. Can you work out how to draw a perfect square that passes through every dot? The secret is to first group the dots into four pairs. Solution overleaf.

Which of the horizontal rectangles do you think is exactly *the same size* as the vertical one? Amazingly, it's actually the central, orange one!

The main part of this building seems to be very distant from the viewer, given the difficulty in making out the stairs in the distance—but if you look closely at the nearest steps you'll see that it's an architectural illusion. The staircase features very shallow steps to create the **illusion of a much larger building**.

Solution to the illusion at the top of the previous page:

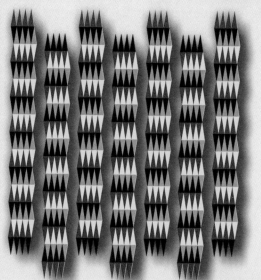

These strips are made up of a relatively simple diamond pattern, but however you look at them they appear to be **sliding up and down** the page!

In this simple image, does the area around the horizontal stripes appear to be **a different shade** or color to that around the vertical stripes? The vertical sections look much brighter than the horizontal sections.

This pattern, constructed from four butterfly
shapes, appears to **shrink inward** into the
center of each butterfly, even as you read this text.
Try looking at the center of one butterfly and then,
when the image stops moving, shift your gaze to
the center of another butterfly, and so on.

The picture below consists of an arrangement of ***spinning*** discs. As you look around the image you should see the discs that you *aren't* directly looking at spinning. This effect is caused by the white highlights.

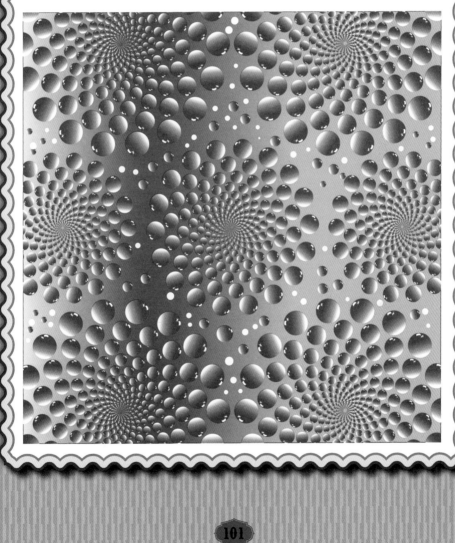

At first glance this picture seems perfectly ordinary, but there's something about the shape that the gull is sitting on that doesn't quite make sense ... The shape at the bottom left consists of two impossible triangles—trace around each triangle to see what's wrong.

This tunnel seems to *shimmer*, the narrower it gets. Despite its simplicity it also conveys an impressive sense of depth.

The center of each of these shapes seems to **glow slightly brighter** than the white paper surrounding it, despite being identical in color.

This ball provides the rather strong impression that it is slowly *deflating* into its center!

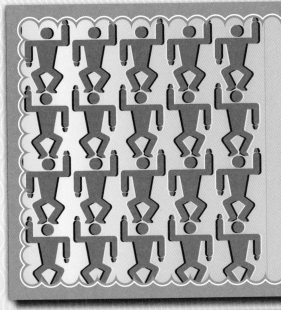

These silhouetted dancers appear to be **swaying** back and forth to an inaudible beat ...

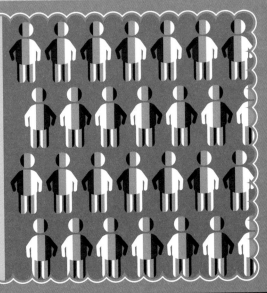

... while these people standing in line are also shifting back and forth to the same silent music.

Stare at this image for a few seconds, then when you move your eyes from dot to dot you should see **glowing, orange-edged dots**.

These red and blue tiles *appear to be sliding* up and down their columns. This effect appears because your brain is desperately trying to line them all up neatly!

The upper red sphere **looks bigger** than the lower one, although in reality they are both printed at exactly the same size. The eye is correcting for the apparent distance variation shown by the checkerboard.

It looks like the right-hand side of this orange shape is at far too low an angle to form a **perfect triangle** with the rest of the visible shape, but this is just an illusion. You can use a ruler to prove that it meets up with the top of the triangle.

Is the cat sitting on a step, or is it *hovering* between stairs? The answer depends on whether you look at the top half or the bottom half of this drawing!

The red square on the right **looks larger** than the red square on the left, but this is only because of the varying size of the surrounding squares. In reality, both red squares are identical.

This *pseudo-3-D* optical illusion was created for an arts show in the Netherlands.

As you move your eyes around this picture, so the balls appear to shift and start to

jostle

for space on the page.

If you're having trouble seeing the illusion, try looking away and then **rapidly shifting** your gaze back. Another method is to look at the center, let your eyes go **slightly out of focus**, then move them around the image in that soft-focus state.

Do you see a large number of black arrows facing down, or a lot of yellow arrows facing up?

This looks like a wire-framed cube, but if you try tracing around the edges you'll soon discover that you'd have **a problem** if you tried adding a solid face to each side!

This **sparkling** arrangement of colored squares
exhibits a curious effect whereby the magenta
squares seem to flicker and change color as
you move your eyes around the pattern.

There appears to be a flowerlike shape in the center of this vibrating, flickering pattern, created through the interference of the narrow lines. This is called a Moiré pattern.

This South American-esque pattern appears to *ripple up and down* as you cast your eyes over it.

This peaceful-looking structure includes a water feature which any gardener would be proud of—a waterfall that *never runs out of water* and doesn't even require a pump to keep it flowing!

This pattern consists of concentric circles of differently colored lighter beads which, combined with darker beads between them, results in the illusion of a **slowly rotating** image.

This illusion combines a rotating center and an expanding outer portion for *a visual double whammy!*

These checkered patterns **don't appear to be quite true** thanks to the overlaid numbers. The top image appears to lean a little, while the bottom image appears to lean at an even greater angle.

Is this a tiny man resting on a hand, or really just someone standing around in the distance?

This illustration **appears to consist** of glowing blue, red, yellow, and green circles, but in fact it's just an illusion! The image is a perfect grid where just the intersections are colored. The circles are imaginary.

These butterflies seem to be **FLYING IN CIRCLES** around a light, just like in reality!

Run your eyes in a vertical direction up and down this pattern, and you will see bands of different shades of green *shift and move* within the image as you do.

This image appears to have two quite **different shades** of green, but in fact there is only one green color. The overlapping white and black lines are creating the effect of there being two shades.

One of these two arrows **appears to be longer** than the other, but in fact both arrows are exactly the same length.

The contrasting centers of these shapes seem to be wanting to swap places, with the white appearing **ultrabright**.

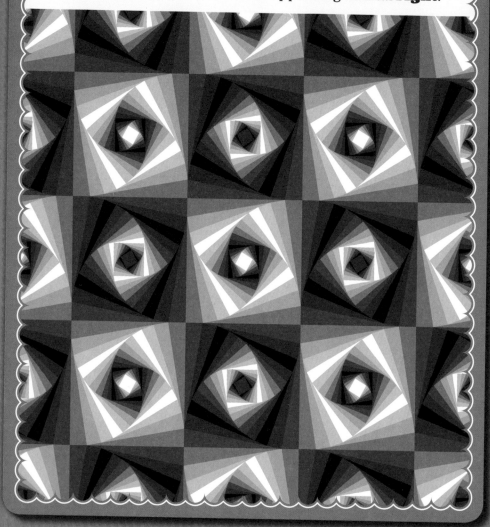

This seems to be a rather boring image, until you start to move the book slowly toward you. As the image moves closer, the blue shapes *start to rotate* around each wheel.

If you tried arranging some dice like this, you'd soon run up against **a substantial problem**! It consists of several impossible triangles grouped inside one larger impossible triangle!

The paper in the center of this image appears to be **tinged with a hint of pale blue**, but it is in fact just as white as the areas away from the center. Your brain is assuming there's a thin blue square overlaying the center.

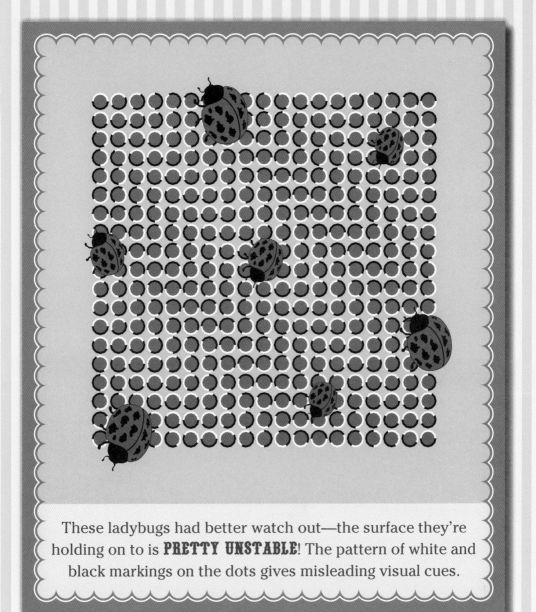

These ladybugs had better watch out—the surface they're holding on to is **PRETTY UNSTABLE**! The pattern of white and black markings on the dots gives misleading visual cues.

Image Credits